MACHINES RULE!

IN SPACE

Steve Parker

Smart Apple Media

Smart Apple Media
P.O. Box 3263
Mankato, Minnesota 56002

Printed in the United States.

Published by arrangement with the Watts Publishing
Group Ltd, London.

Library of Congress Cataloging-in-Publication Data

Parker, Steve, 1976-
  In space / Steve Parker.
       p. cm.—(Machines rule!)
  Includes bibliographical references and index.
  Summary: "Covers a wide selection of machines used in space,
from shuttles to telescopes, outlining how they work and what
they are used for"–Provided by publisher.
  ISBN 978-1-59920-285-3 (hardcover)
  1. Astronautics—Juvenile literature. 2. Outer space–
Exploration—Juvenile literature. I. Title.
  TL793.P32 2010
  629.4–dc22
                                            2008044509

Editor: Jeremy Smith
Design: Billin Design Solutions
Art director: Jonathan Hair
All images copyright © NASA.

Words in **bold** or ***bold italics*** can be found in the glossary on
page 28.

9 8 7 6 5 4 3 2 1

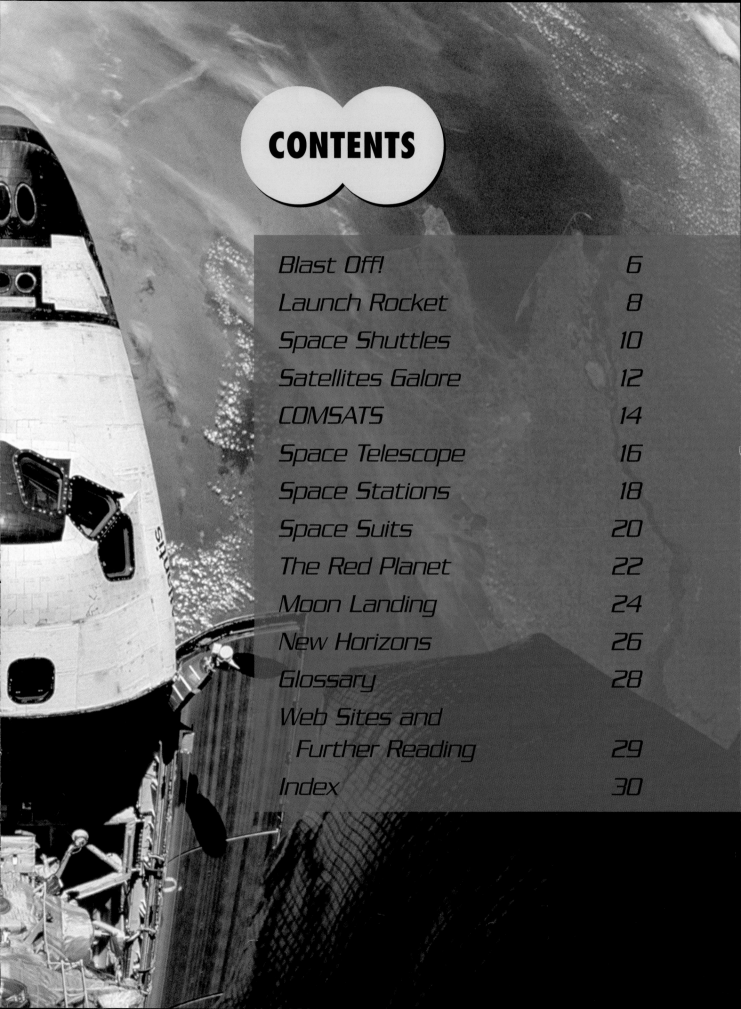

CONTENTS

Blast Off!

We have explored much of our world, but most of space remains unexplored by us. All kinds of machines and crafts travel there. Some help us to understand the mysteries of the universe. Others give us satellite TV!

On the Launch Pad
Rockets are known as **launch vehicles**. They are the biggest, fastest, noisiest moving machines ever made.
They burn tons of fuel each second as they lift all kinds of **payloads** into space, from **satellites** to **space stations**.

Round and Round

Satellites orbit Earth, the Moon, and planets such as Mars and Saturn. They are like our space servants, doing their jobs by remote control as they whiz around in the cold, silent emptiness.

Floating Free

Spacecrafts and machines without people can do lots of tasks in space. But sometimes a human is needed, floating weightless yet safe in a space suit.

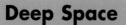

Deep Space

Space **probes** fitted with cameras, detectors, and sensors travel on vast lonely trips to other planets. They send back faint **radio signals** to tell us what they see and find. Then they go deeper into never-ending space, on and on and on.

Launch Rocket

The only engine powerful enough to escape the pull of Earth's gravity is the rocket. It's called a launch vehicle (LV). A "payload" is what's carried into space.

Europe's *Ariane 5* is a "heavy lifter," carrying many tons into orbit. The main part of the rocket contains a giant fuel tank, with the rocket engine at the bottom and the payload in the nose cone.

Massive **solid-fuel** rocket boosters give extra power after launch.

Ariane 5

Operator: European Space Agency

Operator: European Space Agency

Height: 193 ft (59 m)

Width: 17.7 ft (5.4 m)

Payload: 23 tons (21 t) into Low Earth Orbit

First Stage Engine: 1 Vulcain, burn time 7 minutes

Boosters: Solid fuel, burn time 130 seconds

Second stage engine: 1 Aestus, burn time 18 minutes

3 ... 2 ... 1 ... Lift-off! U.S. Atlas rockets have launched more than 80 space missions. The fuel burns in a continuous explosion, thrusting the rocket skywards.

THAT'S INCREDIBLE

To get away from Earth's gravity and reach space, a rocket must travel at least 6.8 miles (11,000 m) per second.

The boosters drop off after launch.

Space Shuttle

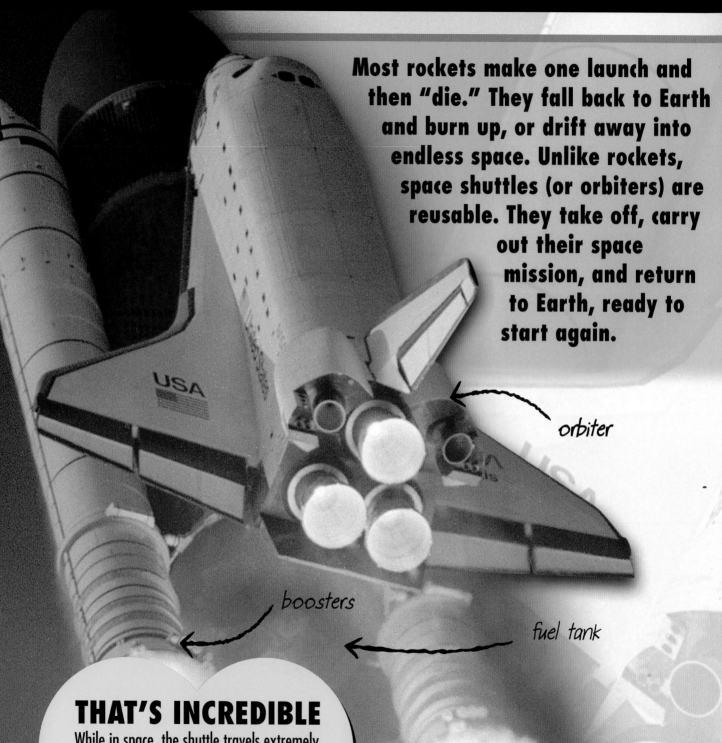

Most rockets make one launch and then "die." They fall back to Earth and burn up, or drift away into endless space. Unlike rockets, space shuttles (or orbiters) are reusable. They take off, carry out their space mission, and return to Earth, ready to start again.

orbiter

boosters

fuel tank

THAT'S INCREDIBLE
While in space, the shuttle travels extremely fast. In fact, the shuttle goes about five miles (eight kilometers) every second.

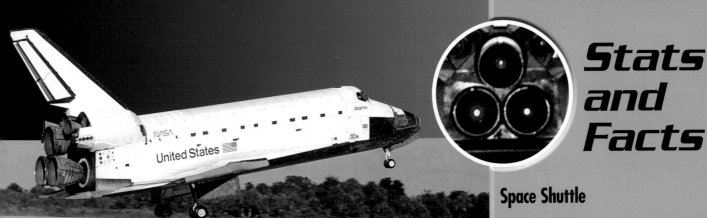

The orbiter comes back to Earth and lands on a runway without engine power. It's the world's biggest glider, touching down at 217 mph (350 km/h).

This shuttle is carrying a satellite back to Earth for repairs.

Space Shuttle

Maker: NASA

Orbiter Length: 122 ft (37.2 m)

Orbiter Wingspan: 78 ft (23.8 m)

Orbiter Height: 149.6 ft (17.9 m)

Orbiter Weight: 121.2 tons (110 t)

Orbiter Engines: 3 Rocketdynes

Booster Height: 149 ft (45.6 m)

Booster Weight: 650 tons (590 t)

Fuel Tank Height: 154.2 ft (47 m)

Fuel Tank Weight: 826.7 tons (750 t)

Complete Takeoff Weight: 2,204 tons (2,000 t)

The crew controls the orbiter using onboard computers. The computers also help them carry out space missions.

11

Satellites Galore

Thousands of satellites orbit planet Earth. They do all kinds of jobs, from helping forecast weather to mapping the land and sea, looking into deep space, and spying on possible enemies below.

Navstars send out radio signals with their position and time to Global Positioning System (GPS) receivers.

solar panel

THAT'S INCREDIBLE

With the best decoder equipment, a GPS receiver can pinpoint its position to the nearest 10 feet (3 m).

Stats and Facts

Navstar Series

Width: Up to 37.4 ft (11.4 m)

Height: 11.1 ft (3.4 m)

Weight: 2.4 tons (2.2 t)

Power: Solar panels generate 1,000 watts (1kW)

Launch Vehicle: Delta

Orbital Height: 12,551 miles (20,200 km)

Orbital Speed: 12.4 ft (3.8 m) per second

Technicians prepare a satellite that will be used to make weather forecasts.

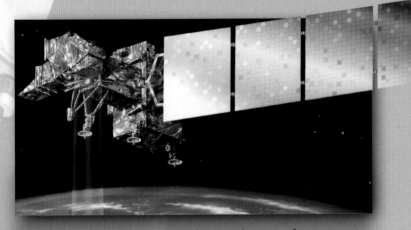

Landsats photograph Earth's surface for map-makers and surveyors. Their powerful cameras photograph overlapping areas of Earth to make up a complete view.

Spy satellites take photographs of buildings from space.

COMSATS

COMSATS are communications satellites. With them we have satellite television, instant phone calls to anywhere in the world, and high speed Internet!

Europe's Artemis satellite sends information through the Earth's atmosphere using a laser beam.

antennas

COMSATS have several dish-like **antennas**. One receives signals to be broadcast from Earth. Another broadcasts signals back down to Earth.

Boeing 376 COMSAT

Purpose: Provide satellite TV

Maker: Hughes

Width: 7.2 ft (2.2 m)

Height: 25.2 ft (7.7 m) including antenna

Launch Date: December 19, 2000

Launch Vehicle: Ariane 5

Weight at Launch: 1.5 tons (1,420 kg)

Weight in Orbit: 0.9 tons (824 kg)

Orbital Height: 39.4 tons (35,800 kg)

The Boeing 376 was the first COMSAT to be launched by the Space Shuttle.

Space Telescope

Telescope
cover door

Mirror
compartment

Instrument
compartment

Why send a telescope into space? High above the surface there are no clouds, no blurring caused by the atmosphere (the layer of air around Earth) and no interference from Earth's lights. It's a clear view, all day, every day.

The Hubble Space Telescope (HST) was launched from the space shuttle in 1990.

THAT'S INCREDIBLE

After Hubble's launch, its mirror was found to be 1/400th of a millimeter out of place. A repair mission costing millions of dollars fixed the problem.

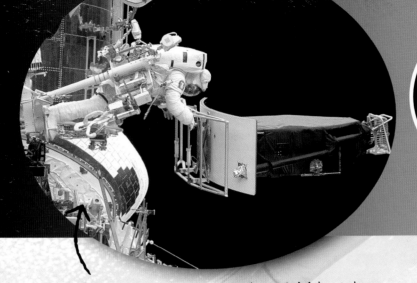

Shuttle astronauts took the Hubble telescope apart to fit in a new, better camera.

Stats and Facts

Hubble Space Telescope

Makers: USA/Europe

Length: 42.9 ft (13.1 m)

Width: 14.1 ft (4.3 m)

Weight 12.2 tons (11.1 t)

Orbital Distance: 366.6 miles (590 km), on average

Orbital Speed: 24,606.3 ft (7,500 m) per second

Orbital Time: 97 minutes

Service missions: 1993 (repair mirror), 1997 (fit new instruments), 1999 (running repairs), 2002 (fit new camera)

This beautiful shot of stars being formed was taken by the Hubble telescope.

The James Webb telescope will be launched around 2013. It will replace the Hubble telescope.

Space Stations

Space stations are built for people to live and work in space. They are built piece by piece. The parts are carried up by space shuttles and rockets. The International Space Station (ISS) is worked on together by many different countries.

THAT'S INCREDIBLE

Russian astronaut Valeri Polyakov holds the record for living in space. In 1995 he stayed on board Mir for 438 days—well over a year!

The space shuttle orbiter Atlantis **docked** with the Russian space station *Mir* in 1995.

International Space Station (ISS)

Makers: Various

Length: 190.2 ft (58 m)

Width: 239.5 ft (73 m) including solar panels

Height: 88.5 ft (27 m)

Weight: 518 tons (470 t)

Orbital Distance: 149.1 miles (240 km)

Orbits per 24 hours: Almost 16

First Crew: in the year 2000

Call Sign: Alpha

The first space station was the US Skylab in 1973, but one of the solar panels fell off at its launch.

solar panel

Space tourists journey to the ISS at a cost of $26 million dollars.

Space shuttle orbiters deliver new parts to the ISS.

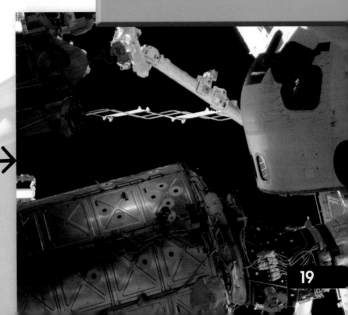

Space Suits

In space there is no air to breathe, and it's freezing cold out of the Sun and boiling hot in it. A space suit keeps an astronaut alive and comfortable for work outside the spacecraft.

THAT'S INCREDIBLE

In a space suit, the innermost layer is the MAG, Maximum Absorption Garment. It's like a soft diaper that soaks up the astronaut's urine.

This astronaut is strapped into the Manned Maneuvring Unit (MMU). It is like an armchair with tiny rocket thrusters.

A space suit has tubes that provide air and cooling water, and has a microphone and headphones in the helmet.

EMU Space Suit

Makers: Various

Suit Weight: 280 lbs (127 kg) on Earth, no weight in space

Suit Cover Thickness: 3/16 of an inch (5 mm)

Number of Layers: 13 including outer cover (1 layer), thermal garment (8 layers), pressure garment (2 layers), cooled undergarment (2 layers)

Undergarment: Temperature controlled by cooled water through 328 ft (100 m) of tubing

Wearing Time: Up to 7 hours

Cost: $12 million per suit

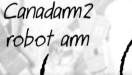

Canadarm2 robot arm

headlights and video camera

safety harness frame

tether straps

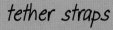

Astronauts in the ISS (see pages 18–19) use space suits when working outside. Tether straps stop them from floating away into space.

The Red Planet

The planet visited most by spacecraft is Mars. It looks red because its rocks and dust contain iron oxide—rust! About 40 missions have set off to Mars, but over half have failed to get there.

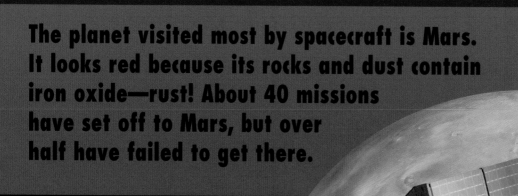

THAT'S INCREDIBLE
Mars **rovers** *Spirit* and *Opportunity* were named by a nine-year-old girl, Sofi Collies, who won an essay competition.

Mars Express went into orbit around the planet on Christmas Day 2003. It has taken thousands of detailed pictures of the mountains, valleys, dust plains and weather.

Stats and Facts

Spirit and **Opportunity**
Twin Mars Rovers

Mission: Mars Exploration Rover

Landing date: January 2004

Length: 5.2 ft (1.6 m)

Width: 7.5 ft (2.3 m)

Height: 4.9 ft (1.5 m)

Weight 396.8 lbs (180 kg)

Power: Solar panels generate 140 watts

Top Speed: 2 inches (5 cm) per second

Average Speed: 3/4 of an inch (1 cm) per second

Drive: 6 electric motors, each turning a 9.8 inch (25 cm) diameter wheel

Two Viking Crafts landed on Mars in 1976, and took pictures like this one.

Two rovers, Spirit (left) and Opportunity, landed there 28 years later.

Moon Landing

Between 1969 and 1972, twelve U.S. astronauts walked on the Moon. They are the only people ever to set foot on another world.

The rocket *Saturn V* blasted off on July 16th, 1969, carrying the spacecraft Apollo 11. The journey to the Moon took four days.

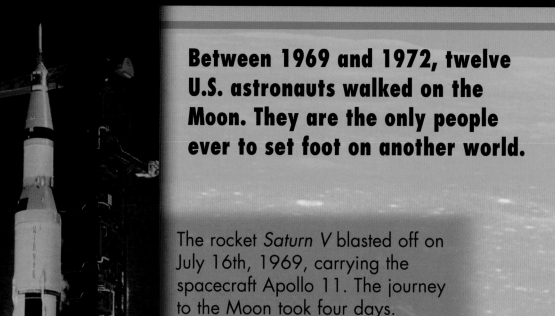

First to set foot on the Moon was Neil Armstrong (center right). He climbed down to the dusty surface, saying: "That's one small step for man, one giant leap for mankind."

Apollo Lunar Module Lander

Name: Apollo 11 *Eagle*

Width: 13.7 ft (4.2 m)

Height: 6.8 ft (6.3 m)

Weight: 16.2 tons (14.7 t)

Crew: Commander, Pilot

Life Support: Three Days

States: Lower descent stage remained on Moon, upper ascent stage blasted back up into Moon orbit

Number Produced: 15

Number landed on the Moon: 6

The Apollo Lunar Module **Lander** Eagle separated from the main spacecraft. It took the astronauts to the Moon's surface before linking up with the rest of the craft again.

antenna for Lunar Module

antenna to the Earth

TV camera

Three Apollo missions took lunar rovers (moon buggies).

THAT'S INCREDIBLE

The Moon has no air, water, or weather. So the astronauts' bootprints in the dust will remain there for thousands of years.

25

New Horizons

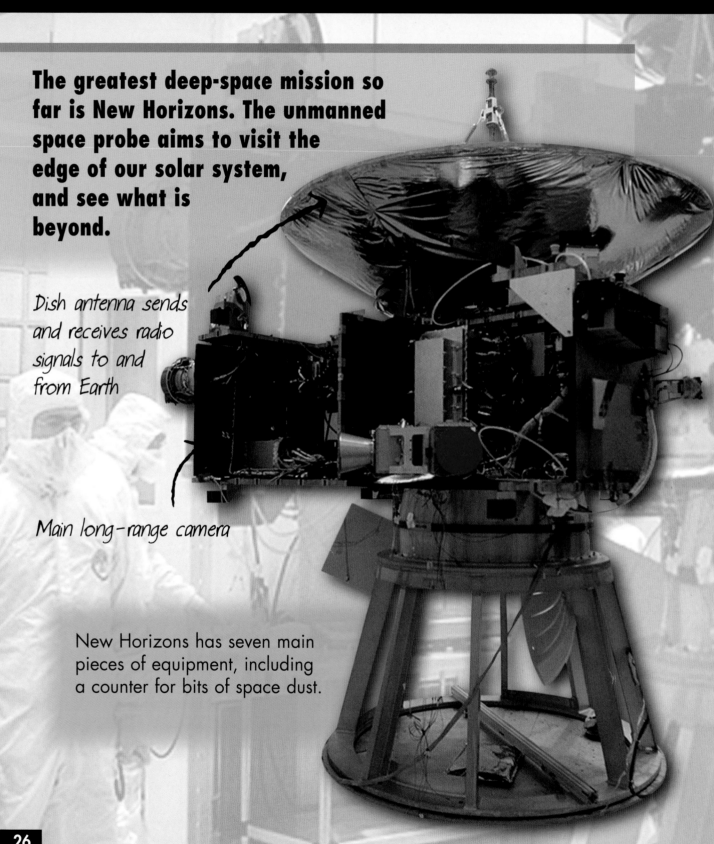

The greatest deep-space mission so far is New Horizons. The unmanned space probe aims to visit the edge of our solar system, and see what is beyond.

Dish antenna sends and receives radio signals to and from Earth

Main long-range camera

New Horizons has seven main pieces of equipment, including a counter for bits of space dust.

THAT'S INCREDIBLE

A radio signal from the Moon takes less than two seconds to reach Earth. When New Horizons reaches Pluto, at the edge of our solar system, its signals will take over four hours.

New Horizons

Operator: NASA

Length: 8.8 ft (2.7 m)

Width: 6.8 ft (2.1 m)

Height: 7.2 ft (2.2 m)

Weight: 1,050 lbs (478 kg)

Launch Date: January 19, 2006

Pluto Flyby: July 14, 2015

Nearest Approach to Pluto: 6,835 miles (11,000 km)

Nearest Approach to Pluto's Moon, Charon: 16,777 miles (27,000 km)

In February 2007, New Horizons flew within 1.4 million miles (2.3 million kilometers) of the biggest planet, Jupiter, with its moon Io in the foreground.

New Horizons took off on an Atlas V rocket at Kennedy Space Center in Florida.

Glossary

Antenna

A device for receiving and sending signals, usually radio or microwave signals. It may be a length of wire or shaped like a rod, dish, or net.

Atmosphere

The blanket-like layer of air (mixture of gases) around Earth, which becomes thinner with height and fades to nothing in space.

Booster

A simple, powerful rocket that gives extra thrust and speed for a short time.

COMSAT

A communications satellite, which receives information as radio waves or microwaves from one part of Earth, and sends it back down to another part.

Dock

To join with another craft in space, usually with an airtight seal so that people and objects can pass from one to the other.

Gravity

The pulling force with which all objects attract each other. It gets greater with size, so Earth has huge gravity, while the Moon's is weaker.

Lander

A craft or vehicle that goes down to the surface of a space object like a planet, moon, comet or asteroid.

Launch vehicle

A rocket-powered craft that goes from Earth's surface into space, usually carrying a payload.

Orbiter

A craft or vehicle that stays in orbit, such as around a planet or moon, while other parts called landers may go down to the surface.

Payload

The cargo, items or goods carried into space by a rocket or launch vehicle.

Probe

A robot exploring craft that has no crew, and travels long distances in space.

Radio signal

Invisible waves of combined electrical and magnetic energy, often used for sending information around Earth and through space.

Rover

A wheeled vehicle that travels across the surface of a planet or moon, either under control of an astronaut or remote control.

Satellite

Any object that goes around another one in space, although the name usually refers to an artificial (man-made) object.

Satellite navigation (satnav)

Using signals from GPS (Global Positioning System) satellites high in space find the location of an object or place.

Solid fuel

Fuel for burning in a rocket or similar engine that is in the form of powder or bricks, rather than liquid.

Space station

A craft where people can stay for a long time as they live and work in space.

Web Sites

http://www.nasa.gov/audience/forkids/kidsclub/flash/index.html

The junior area of the massive website of NASA, the USA's National Aeronautics and Space Administration, which builds and operates many space missions.

http://www.esa.int/esaKIDSen/

Fun interactive site of the European Space Agency with news, games and quizzes on all aspects of space, from the latest rocket launches to the story of the Universe.

http://www.kidsastronomy.com/

Find out about space, the Solar System, stars and galaxies, space travel and much more.

http://www.exploringmars.com/

All about the mysterious "Red Planet" Mars, from the weather to various landers and rovers through the years.

http://www.rivalquest.com/space/

Loads of wonderful pictures about all aspects of space, including the space shuttle and space stations.

Further Reading

Space Technology (How Does It Work?) By Linda Bruce et al, Smart Apple Media, 2007

Space Robots (Robots and Robotics) By Tony Hyland, Smart Apple Media, 2008

Index